Self Heal
(the art of "SIRF HAAN")

Shailja Agarwal

BLUEROSE PUBLISHERS
India | U.K.

Copyright © Shailja Agarwal 2023

All rights reserved by author. No part of this publication may be reproduced, stored in a retrieval system or transmitted in any form or by any means, electronic, mechanical, photocopying, recording or otherwise, without the prior permission of the author. Although every precaution has been taken to verify the accuracy of the information contained herein, the publisher assume no responsibility for any errors or omissions. No liability is assumed for damages that may result from the use of information contained within.

BlueRose Publishers takes no responsibility for any damages, losses, or liabilities that may arise from the use or misuse of the information, products, or services provided in this publication.

For permissions requests or inquiries regarding this publication, please contact:

BLUEROSE PUBLISHERS
www.BlueRoseONE.com
info@bluerosepublishers.com
+91 8882 898 898
+4407342408967

ISBN: 978-93-5628-059-5

Cover design: Shivam
Typesetting: Namrata Saini

First Edition: November 2023

Sparkle which can change your life from depression to bliss, from doubt to faith, from sad state to happy state, from nothing to everything, from pain to ecstasy.

This book is dedicated to mom and my Universe, I am sure my mom turned into an angel once she left in body and brought all opportunities in my life to touch my higher self, My Divine showed me way from time to time. I can't thank Him enough, I can't go further without thanking God's Consciousness, which has completely changed my outlook towards life

About Book: This book came to my mind when in lockdown I could read and learn about different patterns of living which can bring peace and happiness in our life. We can attain happiness by our own efforts without spending any penny on doctors and psychiatrists.

Complete happiness and abundance it can bring by simple ingredients which can be used to remove negativity, different chapters will fill your lives with peace, happiness and fulfilled dreams, Its power packed formula of getting out of depression and negativity, I am very sure that by following different tools, you will bring ultimate happiness in your life. Happy Healing Friends. I am so sure of this because my own life has totally changed after using all of these tools.

Preface

My journey from childhood to young age was filled with my powerful parents, my father was a great visionary and mother was very strong and iron willed lady. We had very interesting childhood with my father and mother who took us to different places for holidays. We three daughters were brought up very powerfully, we were taught driving, being independent, handling ourselves and outdoor affairs. We were brought up to see wider aspects of life, our mother was very religious and pious and very house proud female who brought us up with tender care and concern. Then one day we lost our father who was pillar of strength for us and my mother could not take life without him, she was in grief but still handled everything very strongly. Then one day in 2013, we lost her too, and I think she turned into an ANGEL, maybe she realized real way of living because since she left us, many spiritual paths opened before me, they are still opening and opening. I had become very insecure after loosing

My father then mother, I used to get bouts of anxiety, I tried different practices of self healing.

I came to know slowly and gradually that we are creators of our destiny and I never could believe it till I tried it on myself and they started working, it was tortoise walk but I kept moving towards the path towards fulfillment and now I can say that I am blissful, I live life on my terms, I am totally at peace and I want all other people to come out of pain. But it was not easy journey for me, from 2013 to 2015 I was struggling with my own negativity, fears, insecurities, till the time I started my spiritual journey, I seriously want to share my journey from pain to happy healing of my soul. More power to all unhappy souls. It is simple yet constant effort to search ultimate bliss. But I am sure after applying these simple yet doable tools, you all will come out of your negativity, anxiety, depression because I am healed, happy and blissful by using these tools and wish same for you all.

Chapter 1

Namyo ho renge kyo is first thing that made me fearless and brought me out of anxiety, It's Nichiren Buddhism way of living, it's meaning is: Nam comes from Sanskrit word which means bow down, devote, Nam myo ho renge kyo is thus an oath to touch our own Buddha nature, if we are in our Buddha nature then we are happy, contented and peaceful, you all can try it because chanting this mantra can change vibrations in your body towards positivity, we start experiencing high life state, we start feeling in control of our own selves, we start manifesting our deep rooted desires, happiness is also felt after doing this chant, interested people can Google it for reference that how to do it. You will find lots of success stories, testimonials. People chant nonstop from 15 minutes to 3 hours to manifest their wishes, one can change one's destiny, fulfill all dreams, one thing appealed to me about this practice is that, once a person does follow this chant, he or she is guided from up line or senior person in faith to do kosen rofu which means to find someone in low life state and guide that person about this practice, it's not about your own happiness, people in faith go to that person's house to chant for that person's problem and try to uplift that person's life state. In this time of commerciality, people make a chain of happiness. This is most beautiful thing about this practice, such profound practices are to be revered where people get together to help souls who are little behind in life. Isn't it beautiful in these times of selfishness? Another beautiful thing I liked about this practice is that, disciples are told to make a wish book or Dream Dairy where one gives specific dates to one's dreams by writing positive affirmations to it, they give specific dates to their future dreams as if they have already taken place for example: Thank you Divine for giving me………by this date,….You can fill in the blanks with your desired goal and date, I came to know that by writing your most difficult wishes, they come true, isn't it astonishing? Still I am in daze state as few of my most difficult desires got fulfilled on those specific dates written in my Dream Dairy. Completion of few wishes seemed impossible when I wrote them, but to my astonishment they got fulfilled. This was my first step towards happiness and hope, all over. Everyone out there reading this book, please make a Dream Dairy to make your wishes true. Do you know one thing? writing your dreams of future in affirmation as if they have already taken place was most difficult for most logical person like me, but I came to know after few studies that Universe knows only one thing : to fulfill our desires, and It gives us what we desire, by writing it, we confirm its happening, Universe follows our command but yes it should be good command, not a negative one, or to harm someone, it will never be fulfilled but yes if we have something good in our mind or it's pure desire to have better home, better job, better car because we will be happy to own this, Universe grants it, if by any chance we want to give happiness to world or spread our knowledge to people who need it, then Universe grants our Dream Dairy wishes even faster, it happened in my case, I promised Universe to share my knowledge and happiness to people who are distressed, I am trying to fulfill my promise to My Father: Universe, thank you My Lord for enriching me with knowledge and bliss and abundance of all kind, Thank you Thank You Thank you.

Namyo Ho Renge Kyo brought me out of stupid fears and phobias, made me look inside my own self, made me focused and in control of myself but chanting endless hours was sometimes tedious, but its superb results are amazing, this is beautiful practice , if you guys want, you can give it a try, if it will be your calling, it will change your life, if you are not attracted towards it then I have many more surprises for you, one thing is sure that writing your wishes as mentioned above will help you achieve your goals, you chant Namyo Ho Renge Kyo and make your dream dairy, Universe only knows one thing: To give, grant, manifest, if you think positive it will give you that, if you think negative it will give you negative, it's all Mind Power, wherever your mind goes or thinks of, that is given back to you. It is in your hand to get what you want in life.

Before chapter 2, I would like to tell that I am going to share all things which changed my life, you guys can try all, but one way is more life changing for one person and other thing can be life changer for other person, never ever criticize any spiritual way or practice. One more thing I want to share, that it is not a religion, you can follow your respective religion as you are following because it is not religion, it's lifestyle, it will improve quality of life add loads of happiness, but it's not religion.

Chapter 2

In our house many years back, If something went wrong, mom used to say, God will set it right, She had great faith in God and His Powers. She was regular in going to temple and always I saw her praying, and having strong faith against all odds that things will turn alright. Same thing was inherited which helped me to come out of pain of losing, first father then mother and becoming stronger than ever. But Oct 30 2013,the day we lost our mom, I am sure that she turned into an Angel and kept opening so many positive ways and practices before me that I can say that today I am totally healed, happy, and sorted, I know I have healed myself, and I know I can change lives of others.

After Namyo Ho Renge Kyo, I was quite happy but still sometimes disturbed relationships, many other things were disturbing around me,

Now I came across many studies of positive energies, which are there, but these all negative and positive energies are inside our own selves. We ourselves are game changers. We are our own creators.

These Game Changers Are…

No 1: Salt Magic. Salt has magical properties, it can heal us, we can erase our own negativity by salt.

We have to add a pinch of rock salt to our bathing water or you can rub salt all over body after bath, keep it on for 1 minute then wash it off with water, you will see magical change in your body and mind, you will start functioning positively.

This salt is negativity absorber like a sponge, you must try it to experience it. Another magic of salt is on our relationships, we can keep salt in glass bowl in our washroom, our washrooms are where we excrete negative energy of our body, this salt keeps absorbing all negative energies of our body. This salt bowl has to be changed every month either on no moon day or full moon day, because these two days are very high vibration days, on these days, if you have more of negative energies, you will experience mood swings, irritability, bouts of anger, lots of irritability, and if you are positive being then you will experience peace and happiness. Check your energies on these two days and act accordingly. Do take salt bath on these days as it's very important to cleanse your energies as told previously. Indulge in spiritual practices and put mantra chant CD in your home to bring peace and happiness daily but essentially on these two days.

No moon day is very important day as you can solve many of your blockages on this day, on this day donate in name of your ancestors, like people who left you in body but they still are around you in energy body, I hope you understand what I mean. Like our father, mother, grandparents whoever left us in body. I came to know after few studies that people who leave us in body still want some acknowledgement from us in form of some donation of food, medicines, or any other help to some needy person by taking name of that person that this donation is done for so and so person or you can pray that you are making this donation for all your ancestors, you will experience happiness and calmness, then you can bless me, you may not believe that suddenly you will start experiencing positive changes, miracles in your life. Life turns blissful with their blessings.

I am saying with my own experience. I started using salt in my bathing water and started donating food on no moon day There were too many positive changes in my life, in my house, my surroundings, more happiness, bliss, fulfillment of dreams with these two things only, I would recommend that you all must try these methods to bring happiness in your lives. Change salt bowls kept in your washrooms on no moon day or full moon day. You can throw previous salt in flush, wash the bowl, dry it and keep new salt in it. Full moon day is also very important day, moon is full, energy very high. Donate white things on this day, keep gazing at moon for few minutes and ask moon to give its beautiful energy to you, you will see magical happenings in your life by watching full moon and saying your desires to it, you can try one more thing also, you can make rice kheer (Indian sweet cooked with rice and milk) and keep it in moon light on full moon day, of course covered by thin sieve so that no pests go in it and moonlight transfers to it through sieve, next morning you can give this rice sweet to your family for happiness and positivity it has because of moon rays, I have tried all these things and have experienced positive changes around me, try these small techniques to gain much happiness. Happy Healing to all of readers

Chapter 3

Burning of few things in your house can clear energy of your house, I learnt from a Pranic Healer, take five cardamoms, cinnamon stick, little bit of camphor and some clarified butter then burn all these things and taking it to every room will cleanse energy of house, I have tried it, its really beneficial, you can burn guggal(herb) easily available in India , by adding some mustard seeds and little camphor and burn it to clear energy of house, burning Rose Essential Oil in a diffuser in bedroom or wherever whole family gathers also brings loving energy to home, it clears every negativity from your house, you can put some mantra chants constantly playing in house, for Hindus you can put Gayatri Mantra or Om chant in house to clear negative energy from home, you can burn some good quality incense in house and make a prayer to Divine for peace and happiness, these all healings can be done daily, if not daily then must do on Tuesdays and Saturdays because these are strong days for energy cleaning, you must do on full moon day and no moon day to have peaceful atmosphere in your home, these two days are energy filled days, if you are positive soul, on these days you will be more energy filled, if you are negative person, you will experience more irritation and distress, but if you burn these herbs in house, you will experience more peace and happiness. You will have to tell me if you get some miracles in relationships, arguments, fights or if someone in house is constantly falling sick, or you feel after doing your best you are not earning enough or you are bearing losses, you should do for sure, I will suggest everyone should do it for better life, more happiness and peace. You can burn Sage in your house, this is available on Amazon, this is also good energy cleanser as they are healing herbs. Its smoke can be sent to all rooms by intention to Universe to clear your house from negativity. Be ready for miracles with these small things. Now you and your house will attract all good things. These burning techniques are very effective. Need is to be consistent in your practices, so that you get maximum benefit out of it, you must try it to experience it's magical results.

Chapter 4

POWER OF GRATITUDE

Power of gratitude is so vast that we need volumes to write on it, one single human being can't understand it's amazing results, it can completely transform your life, since childhood we have been taught by our elders that we should keep thanking God for smallest things in our life, but I never understood its life changing results till I was told by one of my mentors to keep paying gratitude to most tiniest thing in my life, I used to think that its taught as we are taught in childhood to greet people who visit our homes and saying thank you to God was general teaching, but when I was told to do it as ritual then I did it just because my mentor said to do, but later I understood from this simple yet practical person whose teachings are so very simple yet result oriented. She taught that for being thankful for things which we already have, we can attract big fortune because Law of Abundance says if we thank the money, clothes, our body, our house, each person in our life even though negative one, we attract more fortune, more money, bigger house, bigger car but first we have to be thankful for what we already have. Can you believe? Even I could not till I gave it a try, still am trying but results are amazing. I started thanking even smallest thing in my life, example: my body, its each part, my mind, my family, difficult people in my life, my parents, my siblings, friends who are no more my friends, who hurt me, who created obstacles, because they brought me closer to my spiritual practices, because of uneasy people I came closer to my manifestation. I have understood power of gratitude, I know that if I am thankful then Law of Universe will bring more situations for me to be thankful for. I am thankful to Universe that I am able to write this book, which will change lives of many people, one just have to be thankful for all the things which we already have in our lives and experience it's positive effects, what is your loss in trying and no special task, just being thankful in your mind, just give it a try and see miracles happening in your life, but what is our normal behavior? We see only lack, ten good things will happen, we will not appreciate but one negative thing happens, we start cribbing, we see someone good looking and slim, we start criticizing our body, we start saying that what I have done that I am not beautiful, I don't have good parents, good siblings, good spouse, my house isn't good, I am not travelling as much my friend is doing, my staff is not so good. Just accept that all of us do that, by doing so what we are gaining? Actually nothing at all, except pain, even I used to do all this till the day I understood power of being thankful, I came to know that by being critical I was attracting only misfortune, then I thought of giving it a try, I started practicing it by deliberation, though I lacked at it all the time, but kept on trying. I started seeing changes in my life, people around me. I started attracting abundance, I started getting opportunities, travel, family happiness, I was leading unhappy life, which is changed into happy, contented life.

If I have difficult relation in my life, I thank that person because that person is trigger towards my spiritual growth, my ultimate happiness. I really love difficult people of my life because they brought me to next level of self growth, happiness in life. This is 100 percent correct that when we start thanking for the things which we already have in life then Universe blesses us 1000 fold.

Actually no one teaches this, I sincerely believe it should be taught in schools and universities, we study so hard, then work so hard, then earn with so much hard work, then we crib so much for becoming so hard and still not as happy and satisfied with life as we dreamt once for ourselves. We should do all hard work but start doing our gratitude practice along with, then start seeing changes which lead us towards positivity, we should thank Universe for the things which are on its way, events which are yet to take place, Universe is so kind that it grants us all that we desire

Actually it is so simple practice that we have to be grateful in mind for all things we desire for, in advance. Universe knows nothing else than giving us what we ask for. But human mind seeks difficult solutions like going to counselors, experts, human beings think that they are very intelligent, and they use their logical minds, but what happens in return? They complicate their problem more and more, because when we discuss negative thoughts, these thoughts multiply because Universe knows only, to give back to us, what we think of.

My dear friend why can't you try this simple magic of gratitude? If you gain something, it will be good for you, if you don't gain then you can give more time to the practice of gratitude. You will surely have beautiful life. Just pay gratitude in advance for things which we desire for, if you get those things, bless me and you can spread this practice of happiness to other unhappy souls .You will actually get all these things but you will have to practice gratitude for long time to get results, not so long but at least for some time, then see how Universe changes your life, pouring blessings in different forms, different manner, but we must be receptive of hints and signs of Universe's blessings, So start being grateful for very small thing too.

Stop using reasoning of your mind, your logic, your intelligence. But on my advice only once use this magic of gratitude, see everything moving towards perfect way which will lead us to the path of immense happiness and great success, I shall give you few examples: If your staff isn't good according to your logical mind, then start being grateful that at least you can afford staff, because of this staff, you can handle things better. Many don't even earn enough to meet two ends meet, leave aside owning staff, you will see with this practice of gratitude you will sow seeds of success, fulfillment of your dreams. With conscious mind and constant practice you will change your most difficult karma, If your spouse isn't good or supportive then you say Thank You to Universe that you have spouse, many are there still unmarried or have lost their spouses, be in gratitude that you could at least experience marriage, Universe in return will soften your spouse towards you, what was your task in it? You were only being grateful. It is actually so simple. But we make it complicated by our logics. Many of you, reading this feel astonished to read this, how is it possible, but my dear friend, what is your loss in trying this? Don't try it for 4-5 days and expect results, but practice it at least for a month for best results without spending a single penny, without wasting your precious time. Sitting in bedroom or lounge you can practice it in your mind, and see magical results in return, by doing nothing actually, I would recommend that you should try it and one try will not be sufficient because our logical mind which is always chattering will pull us back in web of misfortune by bringing us back to thoughts of lack, we have to master our mind by constant practice so that we manifest our all dreams,

I would recommend that you make a gratitude journal, in which daily you can write your 10 blessings for which you are grateful in life. It can be your body, mind, home, your car, anything that comes to your mind, you can keep adding new or repeat same but please do it to believe it because it will bring you close to your manifestation. In day time, when you walk in the house you can repeat your blessings in your mind, you will start having miracles in your life.

Happy Fortunate Life to all of you from my side, only by being grateful for what you already possess and for what you desire for, in advance, to Universe, you can get it .

Thank you for reading it and changing mine and yours life

Chapter 5

POWER OF POSITIVE AFFIRMATIONS

I am sure when my mom left her body in 2013, She turned into an angel and guided me slowly and gradually

Now I will tell you how you can change your life towards path of happiness. By speaking all positive things about your future, energy flows towards your positive affirmations. Example:

I say:

I am totally happy

I am super rich

I am miracle, all good things come to me.

I am super healthy

I have abundance

I am money magnet

My Universe loves me and works for me

Money keeps coming to me when required

My relationships are beautiful

And so on.....you can make your own affirmations by saying a phrase 15 to 20 times or more, you will start seeing your dreams come true. Power of positive sentences is tried and tested by many souls, one has to just keep repeating these sentences many times to realize your dreams, Law of Attraction starts attracting that very thing which you speak repeatedly, it's all game of subconscious mind, whatever your subconscious mind will hold that thing will materialize, so we have to train our subconscious mind that we are getting our desire fulfilled by these positive affirmations, you will start seeing results of taming this subconscious mind of yours. You can create your own affirmations according to your heart's desire, but beware: Don't create or speak any negative affirmations, because you will stand nowhere and you will attract misfortune.

Whatever you wish, make affirmation for that wish, keep chanting that affirmation as many times as you can, while walking, driving, sitting, watching television, doing your daily chores, magic is actually within but we keep searching it outside, we will do all tough things for fulfilling our dreams but will not apply this small magic. Actually Universe is very kind and giving and it hears us and manifests what we speak. If we speak good, it will manifest good, if we speak bad it will manifest bad. We are our own masters, we don't need to step out of house and work hard for achieving what we want, only small things are needed but consistently. These affirmations have brought many beautiful changes in my life, so I expect same for you all but one thing is certain that you should believe it that those affirmations will take place. You should try it with positive mind state to have fulfillment of those affirmations

Best time to speak these affirmations is early morning, when you wake up, because at that time our subconscious mind is very active and whatever is spoken straight goes into subconscious mind and it starts taking place, second best time is when you are about to sleep, this time is also very powerful for our subconscious mind. We keep moving with our conscious mind and believe in all logics but whole power is with our subconscious mind, once we activate this, this is the time miracles will start happening. We actually need to work on ourselves but we keep searching solutions outside. We blame people, places and situations for our problems but will not try anything new to our ears!!! We need to tame our subconscious mind, not see with conscious mind, while we see with conscious mind, we start using logic, how is it possible that I can get this or that while my situation is bad, I am poor, my job is not stable. Yes it might be your reality but you have to feed all miracles you have inside you to your subconscious mind. On my advice please try this in early morning and at night before sleep, or you can write these affirmations before sleep because writing makes it into reality faster, in your gratitude journal you can write these affirmations too. Do it for one month and you will experience miracles in your life.

Chapter 6

FORGIVENESS FOR YOUR OWN PEACE

I Thank my mentor for this beautiful technique, We all have one or other relation in our life which is most troublesome, It can be spouse, parent, sibling, partner, parent in laws and so on. We all are here to solve one major relation in our life which always create hurdles in our life, now what we generally do? We argue, we fight, we plot, we plan to overcome that person and problems created by that person, what happens? We think we have taken 5 steps ahead, next moment we take 7 steps back, is it not? How much we try our best but we are unable to crack this problem and fix this irritating person, daily new situations occur, new hurdles by this person, we fight back, we fall on our back, more we fight, more we fall!! Now all of you must be thinking that what is the solution?

Solution my dear friend is within our own selves, you are born to solve this relationship. Make it peaceful, or make amends.

Actually we choose our relations before our birth, we had troubled that particular soul in our past incarnations, now you will not believe it ! But try this forgiveness technique, for which you don't need to spend a single penny on it, only thing is 5 to 10 minutes of doing daily practice of forgiveness prayers. For more difficult relation, do it constantly for 21 days minimum and after that keep doing whenever you feel like, even if you are a non believer of such things like past birth etc, still I will advice you that give it try for your own peace and happiness, once you see it's magical outcome, if you resolve your negative relationship then stay in happiness and peace and bless me. If you feel that you have not resolved it yet then try it again, it is a tried and tested technique, some difficult relationships are solved in 21 days, some take little longer time, sometimes it comes to mind of logical person that why should be forgiveness prayers done by a person who is receiving difficult time from the person, who is torture some, difficult, but you must understand who is getting trouble ? One who is giving problem or one who is receiving? One may think that why should such practice be done while mind is saying to curse and abuse that tormenting demon? Even I used to think like this but once a person understands the value of one's own peace, happiness and growth and you don't want this person to torture you for your whole life, once you have Divine wisdom to attain peace and ultimate bliss then you will definitely do this wonderful practice. Don't get disheartened, because you will see miracles happening around you, you will see flexibility in that person, you will feel as if you have tamed that person! Isn't it beautiful indeed? You will have to stop your blabbering mind which will stop you from doing it. Because negative forces do not want you to come out of your negativity, you will have to use your Divine wisdom, literally asking for it from Universe. In some cases relationship becomes beautiful and fruitful, in some cases it vanishes from your life, in some cases relationship becomes useful for us, I have tried it and tested it, it is actually amazing, life changing, fruitful and progressive for your physical, mental and spiritual growth.

But what happens when we are told to do forgiveness prayers? We find it most difficult to forgive a person who gave us ultimate pain, There is block of ego, hurt, reasoning in our mind that why should we forgive this person at all!!But do we know that we are blocking our own happiness! You ask yourself a question that what is there to lose by doing this.

If you sort this relation then you will become happy and peaceful, what is forgiveness prayer actually? We have to visualize that person and say:

I seek forgiveness from the souls of this life and past lives,

Whom I may have harmed knowingly or unknowingly

I love you, I respect you. I seek forgiveness from you

Thank you for forgiving me

I forgive the souls of this life and past lives who may have harmed me knowingly or unknowingly

I love you, I respect you. I forgive you,

Thank you for accepting my forgiveness

I forgive my own self for, sometimes

I may have been unkind to my own self

I love myself

I respect myself

I forgive myself

Doing this forgiveness prayer takes your 5 minutes daily but it will give you 100 fold, and life time of happiness ahead. We have to crack one most difficult relation in our life 1st then we can try for other difficult relationships in our life, You can keep doing till the time you start feeling softening of that person, once you experience it, you will start feeling blessed and do bless me at that time. For relationships we need to visualize that person while doing Forgiveness Prayers, for other issues like not getting a chid or not getting married or financial instability we can do it towards Our Divine or Universe, we will start seeing amazing results after doing it. This is Divine Way Of Living, once you sort your relations then try touching other lives around you, you will feel more blessed and keep this chain of happiness going by giving it to others this chain of blessings will increase more blessings in your life. If we don't solve this particular relationship in this lifetime, we will keep meeting such people and facing such situations in our future incarnations. If you don't pass out first class, how will you go to 2nd one? You will keep failing and keep solving same problem again and again. Many families have same type of karma from generation to generation. Their past generations too have same type of problems like not having a child or strained relations amongst relatives. Many have children who don't get married or children have same kind of physical ailments, these are outcome of some misdeeds done by some past generations. You can break this chain by only forgiveness prayers, one simple thing done by you will break curse for future generations. One must at least give it a try for oneself and to help others, and to move towards a life of peace and happiness, one more important thing is that you don't need to personally go to that person and ask for forgiveness, because in reality that person also does not remember anything, this is only soul to soul talk, it's actually on energy level, and that person's behave will change towards you for sure, or situation will change for you completely, try it my friend, I give you guarantee that you will have most beautiful experience of lifetime.

Chapter 7

STEPPING BACK

This tool is so very beautiful that volumes can be written on it, what it means by stepping back. It means when we face any situation where we feel uncomfortable or we face any bad scene with someone, what do we do usually? We argue, we put our point strongly, we raise our voice, we shout, to gain attention, but what happens? We lose our relation, we lose our peace, our energy gets depleted because of anger we have towards that person, now in this situation what should be done? We should use tool of stepping back, it means moving away from that place physically, wash your face, go for a walk if possible, otherwise go to plants or near nature, talk to nature or you can open your palms towards sky and talk your point of view to Universe, may be you will not believe how by talking to open sky or to Universe, our all problems are moved towards solutions!! Universe gives you new more powerful situations and opportunities, power over the problem, now you have power, not others, you are the boss. I never could understand this stepping back till I tried it. Instead of putting your point in that heated moment, one should step back from that situation, do as told earlier, talk to your Divine in open space as we talk to our father, you will see that a new situation is created for you, you have dissolved that negative moment, actually it may sound weird to many souls but believe me once, my friend, that Universe listens, and grants solution to your problem and peace to you, doors of new kind of happiness will open before you, miracles will start taking place in your life, you may talk to that person later, on same problem but when both are logical, when you have given some time in between that situation, but do not let anyone spoil your peace of mind with their words and actions. By stepping back literally, you will understand the situation better, by talking to Universe, it will give some amazing solutions. You may voice out your point when situation is calmer, other person will be receptive too.

When you step back, if done consciously, you may see a new moment is created. Now visualize a new moment which you want to create. Whatever new moment you will visualize, will start taking place, you can enjoy this new moment which you visualized only by one tool: Stepping Back, actually you stop yourself from becoming puppet in other person's hand, who tries to provoke you for pleasure. You become master of your destiny. Have you come across a person who does not respond to any provoking? If you know such person you must be knowing how irritating it is!! The person who is not responding to provocation has actually mastered The Art Of Stepping Back. You recreate a new moment by not responding to negativity, this new moment will recreate your destiny, rather you will create your own destiny. Happy Stepping Back My friends

Chapter 8

HIGHER SELF

What is higher self ?higher self is our best version, peaceful, filled with love, every person has two shades of character, one is lower self one is higher self. Life takes us daily to new situations, which lead us to experience both side of our personality. When we feel humbled, satisfied, calm, quite, giving, then we are in our higher self. When we are jealous, critical, malicious, create drama, when we are mean then we are in our lower self. When we abuse, hit, create scenes, then we are at our lowest selves. Now to lead a fruitful life what do we do? We have experienced our both selves at some time or other, we actually want to be in our best version always but our darker side touches us more often. When we have to talk to someone important or attend a meeting, we just need to steal a moment for ourselves and say that my higher self please connect to other person's higher self, Divine is so pure and benevolent that by just putting our intention, we can touch other person's better version, I have resolved many of my arguments by just calling my own and other person's higher self

Just think how simple is this!! To call only once and just like a Jinnie, our Divine, our loving father awakens our better version and other person's too, with whom we have arguments or difference of opinion, this will help you in family disputes or any other kind of inter connective communicative problems but yes one has to be aware at that moment to connect with our Divine and call our higher self, If you are not aware and you forget to call Divine for connection then don't blame me, because Universe is very simple, it works on our thoughts, if you forget and call in between the conversation when you remembered even then it will work.

Is it not simply amazing that magic wand is with us only, we just have to use at right time, right place, I have tried each of technique and have experienced bliss, that's why I am sharing this beautiful knowledge, way of living. Higher self is always as pure as Divine Himself, so we connect to persons, places and things like Divine would have done, actually life is amazingly beautiful since I have learnt all magical tricks, so I want all of you to experience blissful, peaceful, most beautiful life. I would like my Divine at this moment to connect my higher self with all reader's higher self and ask Divine to help each one of you to come out of any lower state of mind with the help of this technique, and pass it on so that this chain of beautiful experience never breaks

May your higher self always guide you all through your life.

Amen

Chapter 9

GUARDIAN ANGELS

How many times have you heard this word Guardian Angels? You all will say : many times, but how many of us know that each one us on this planet is born with two guardian angels, This may sound strange but each person is assigned by Lord, two personal angels for our assistance, they come on our beck and call, but you will ask where are they? Why can' we see them? All of these questions may arise, and they are natural to arise. Answer to that is, they are near your aura and always ready to help us, but one thing is clear that that they do not come to help till we don't call them to help, if you call them for any problem like : My guardian angels please come and help me come out of this difficult situation, please help me, assist me to finish so and so task, you will experience that for whatever you called them for, is done, solved, fulfilled, to your utter astonishment, task is done in best manner ever known. When I studied about it, I too was astonished and have been trying it ever since, strangely my works are being done, arguments solved, wishes fulfilled, problems vanished, right thing at right time is done. You guys can give it a try when you are planning to make a deal with someone or even when you are planning to go for some business or job, you may laugh but you must understand that getting for right deal is also very important, your money is important which spent on that venture you may sometimes miss a deal and you may think : I called my angels even then I missed it, you must take it like this that angels didn't want this deal, it may not be good for you, if you went for some deal asked assistance of guardian angels, and couldn't make that deal, please take a signal to stop, and in few days time, you may see that you have cracked amazing deal than the one you missed, you will deal for better, in future, they don't allow you to do wrong deal and wrong shopping, it is like your father holding your hand from doing wrong thing. I myself have handed over my major decision making, in hands of my guardian angels and I am cracking most fruitful deals and getting lots of benefits, but yes initially you will have to totally trust whatever comes at that particular moment. You may sometimes think at that particular moment that you are facing loss, but if you trust your angels you will find that miracles are happening in your life, one has to call one's angels. I will give you an example: My friend had gone to crack a deal which seemed at that time very good to my friend but it was not appealing to me at that time, though it seemed very luring to my friend. I asked him to call his guardian angels and ask them if the deal was good then it may take place. My friend did not believe in all these things and was quite irritated and confused, but on my asking he connected with guardian angels and he called me that deal was done, the terms did not sound good to me but I told him to surrender to Divine Plan because of my trust.

Next morning final payment and paper work was to be done. Next morning my friend called me to tell that person with whom deal was being done asked my friend to do full payment in advance then stocks will be shown and payment was not very small amount and that person said that if some stocks are not of good quality even then stocks had to be taken, My friend got irritated by unreasonable terms and stubbornness of that person and reasoned with him that without seeing stocks how could he make full payment, he refused to make deal and came back, for few days he was very much depressed because so much time and energy wasted and nothing gained! But I was very sure from inside that he was saved from a situation he would have regretted. I consoled him and after few days he got much better deal in much lesser rate, then he got very happy, I asked him to trust his angels. Is it not amazing? I would request you all that hand over your problems, troubles and doubts, business deals relationships or any kind of alliance to your guardian angels and totally trust them. What may not sound good to you may be best in end. You carry on your work and do hard work as well towards your dreams but hand over the outcome to your guardian angels, they will serve you, help you, protect you, love you, pamper you like a parent, need is only to ask them, call them, If you do not ask they do not come to assist.

From today onwards take their help in every situation, make it your life style to ask for their help in every little thing in life, you will start feeling loved, protected, guided, and getting best things in best way, you will start getting help from odd places, unexpected profits, everything turning your way. How magically beautiful your life will become !!

You can at least try it because you have nothing to spend, nothing to lose, but everything to gain only.

Happy Guardian Angel filled life ahead my dear friends !!

Chapter 10

CONSCIENCE LIVING

Watching what you are doing or watching your breath leads to conscience living, I heard this word from my mentor and couldn't understand it's meaning but gradually understood that it's most beautiful experience, it's kind of meditation. It's to watch constantly what you are doing, what you are eating, watching each morsel of food while eating, seeing and enjoying each sip of your drink which is going inside you, I was very absent minded whole of my life, keeping my belongings here and there and then bringing down whole cupboard to search that thing, then putting things back, same patterns again and again, but I could not understand anything because mind was not doing anything consciously. When I learnt about this way of living, I understood it's beauty, it's like prayer, I know what I am doing, watching each moment of my life, enjoying each sip of my tea. I am much more organized, keeping things in place, I am not loosing keys and other belongings here and there, still learning a lot, yet sorting things, I am in better command of my own self, otherwise living was haywire. It was frustrating to live mindlessly, now life is much sorted, negative patterns are broken, I live, speak, walk, plan my day according to my wish, my command. I know what I am doing, am at peace and usually filled with excitement and joy, when you live mindfully then you live actual life. You achieve what you want to achieve because you are alignment with your Divine. Many may ask how to do it? I will explain it to you all in most simple way, just watch your breath whenever you are free, then it will convert in to a habit, watch your each breath going inside then seeing each breath going out, by doing this you will start living mindfully, many times you may forget to do it, never mind, when you remember it, at that point do it, till it becomes a natural thing to be done, and good habits cultivated are gift of life, life will start blooming once you start living mindfully, once you experience it you would love to experience it again and again. We are taught many things in schools and universities but these things are no where taught. I believe that these all practices should be added in study course of every child, life will turn beautiful and worth living. I will try in my life to try that these practices should be added from school level. Each human being should lead empowered life, full of positivity, full of peace. Happy Conscious Living all beautiful souls. When experienced conscious living, by anyone then that person actually starts enjoying life, each breath is prayer, each activity is religion, each action is bliss because you do everything with an awareness which is spiritual actually. A person with conscious living lives fruitful life which is filled with joy and feeling of fulfillment, one becomes confident of one's actions and feeling of satisfaction is always there. So I would suggest everyone that one must watch one's breath which is actually meditation in itself and which brings lots of satisfaction to the person.

Chapter 11

GOLDEN BALL EFFECT

This Golden Ball of Divine Magic is actually magical tool given by God's Consciousness group. This is magical tool Golden Ball, This is actually visualizing oneself in Divine Protection and feeling at ease seeing oneself and ones important things in protective Golden Ball. Many miracles are there of this Golden Ball. So many people are benefitted by this awesome tool. How to use this magical tool?

One simply has to visualize the item you have lost for long time, or you lost it few days back, you just have to see that item in Golden Ball, you will be amazed that you will get lost thing in short time or sometimes it may take some time to get this lost thing, but usually it's found in no time, rather people have reported to get something else which was lost long time back, also found along with recently lost thing. There are testimonials regarding this on God's Consciousness page FB. I was shocked in positive daze after reading about this, more dazed after using it literally 100 times and I have succeeded nearly all times. if you had an argument with someone you wanted to have peace with, you can visualize that person with yourself in Golden Ball, laughing and having good times, you will be astonished it will turn out like this, if you don't want yourself to be indulged in conversation with a person whom you don't like at all, you can see yourself in Golden Ball, you will see that you are saved from that person's negative aura, this is beautiful Divine Tool. Golden Ball is actually used by all kind of people, for visualizing their things, their relationships, their dreams, their house, cars, food, even business and everyone has reported victory. Isn't it shocking? But you will be pleasantly surprised to know it's magical effects You can use it to believe it but yes, use it for positive thing not for anything negative, otherwise it will be rubber band effect, like you pull rubber band and when you leave it, it comes back to you only, if you can do it with positive frame of mind, please try, put your future dreams in Golden Ball and sit and visualize it for at least 5 minutes like a reel going in your mind, you will see slowly and gradually your dreams will start moving towards manifestation, in few years you will find that you have many fulfilled dreams.

If you have some business meeting with rivals or some where you want peaceful negotiations, you can try this tool by watching yourself with that person in Golden Ball, having positive interaction or whatever you wish for, you may feel amazed by it's miraculous results. You may feel like you have a fairy's magic wand with you, with which you can fulfill your desires and dreams. It may sound weird to some logical souls, as at one point I too used my rational brain that how can it be possible? But once you start having trust and you start trusting your Divine then you surrender and without questioning start using such tools, you may start having surprises and miracles in your life, when you have positive surprises around you then you start trusting more and very likely to have more miracles. Does it not sound like a dream? Actually it is a dream come true, all above practices if followed correctly and mind fully, you are bound to have pleasant surprise all around you, my dear readers please use this beautiful tool for your lost things, for your protection, for your house, for fulfillment of your dreams, your strained relationships, your children, your money, your car, everything can be put in Divine Golden

Ball. You can put any situation which you want solution for can be seen in Golden Ball, the solution can be seen in Golden Ball nearly every time outcome is very positive. If we start following these Divine Paths without any reasoning, we will see so much happiness, solution based problems, fulfilled dreams but you have to constantly follow these beautiful life changing tools to experience life full of tingling fun filled moments.

Readers I would advice all of you to give it a try to see magical changes in your life. You will definitely bless me because your life will take 360 degree positive change.

Chapter 12

IMPORTANCE OF FOCUS

You will not believe me that how focus can change your life, when I came to about it, I understood that where ever our focus goes that thing expands, means if we focus that we are happy, healthy and prosperous we start becoming all that on what we put our focus upon, sometimes we have argument and strained relationship with someone then our focus goes to that strained relationship and we weave so much against that, person or situation, we create a story of our own and see whole outcome too, how that person or situation will harm us, without thinking that maybe whatever we have woven or created in our mind is all fake, but because whatever we have put our focus upon increases, expands so whatever we have imagined or woven starts taking place and we rejoice that we knew it already or start trusting our intuition, but actually when we were focusing on negative outcome of that situation, if we would have shifted our focus to positive outcome of that situation, you will see everything into positive, not only see but things will start moving in positive direction, things will start taking place because wherever focus goes that thing grows, it's all game of mind, if we let our mind play it's games, we lose because mind doesn't let you see positive easily, if we take our mind, and consciously sow and weave happiness and positivity, don't let negative thoughts take over, we will win the game and have all fulfilled dreams but even masters fail sometimes, and negativity overtakes a person's positive weaving, but we have to do it deliberately, by effort, we should immediately shift our focus on some good that happened in past, or some imaginary good that we ever imagined in dream, feel as it has already taken place or happened, you will realize that whatever positive you thought, has started taking place. This is itself so beautiful that all your dreams will come true.

This book and words of it are not mine, I was guided by some Divine Force to write it and I am writing it, may each person who reads it gain many fold out of life. May my Guardian Angels always guide me to do best for others, and receive best for my self and others. God bless all beautiful souls with enlightened life. Now I would recommend that whenever you get time or you remember, start focusing on good around you, imagine good things happening to you and good will start taking place. Amen!!

Chapter 13

CHAKRA HEALING.

I came to know about chakra healing importance only few years back, what role does it play in one's life is actually astonishing, will a person without awareness of this ever understand that all our life problems are connected with our chakras? Our money issues, insecurity towards future, our fears and phobias, our passion about our dreams, our creativity, our behavior towards others, even others behavior towards us is all connected to our chakras. It's actually Pandora's Box opening if you understand that Chakra Healing is actually door to our happiness. Fulfillment of all desires and dreams. Actually I could not believe it till I tried it and this book is being written after my chakra healing practice. I shall give you brief knowledge of different chakras and their functions for our life purpose, our growth, we shall start with:

Root Chakra: It is located at base of our spine, the start of genitals and most of times we have it blocked and energy does not move upwards and we get stuck in our material needs, in fulfilling our basic needs for survival ; FOOD, CLOTH and SHELTER. Once we keep worrying about these aspects, how can we do anything for society for our nation, for our own life purpose!!!It plays a vital role in our physical wellbeing, our all ailments are connected with different energy points located in our body, our emotional problems are also connected with chakras blockage, our financial problems are also connected with chakra balancing, can you believe only 5 minutes of daily practice can bring miraculous results in all aspects of our life. Why we are not doing it is only because of lack of faith, lack of awareness, lack of knowledge, lack of self drive, if by any chance we train ourselves for such practices then we will enjoy best life!! Root Chakra is actually root of our being, either filled with happiness and security or filled with fear, insecurity and unhappiness, legs pain, knees pain when this chakra is blocked, we should grease this chakra, speak Lam, talk to the junction as if talking to a friend, it's color is red, its mantra is LAM, healing of Root Chakra is very important.

Sacral Chakra: This is located 2 inch below navel, its connected with our self esteem and our will power.

When it is blocked you blame persons, places and things for your situation, ailments related to this is kidney problem, urine related issues, emotional issues, sexual problems, lack of energy, all are related to this chakra, and when it is healed then one is excited about small things in life, your passion awakens, your creativity awakens, you follow your passion, it's color is orange and mantra is VAM grease it, talk to it and speak vam, visualize orange color there at 2 inch below navel, your whole being depends on it . You need to heal it to achieve anything in life, having healthy kidneys, having good sexual life.

Solar Plax Chakra: This chakra is located at navel point and surrounding area, body parts related with it are liver, gall bladder, pancreas. Emotions attached are: Ego, passion, lack of confidence, obesity, skin disease, feeling that others are controlling you, what others think disturbs you a lot, stomach related issues, ulcers, conception issues, all are related with this chakra, grease this chakra, talk to it, open this junction by chanting mantra RAM. It's color is yellow, healing is very important for these 3 chakras to have fruitful life. Good things related with chakras are: name, fame, glory, financial abundance all are achieved with this chakra healing.

Heart Chakra: This is located at centre of chest, color of this chakra is green, it is centre of all chakras, this is center of love, one's ability to love others and one self, when it is blocked, one feels unworthy of love, feels sorry for oneself, unable to let go, forgiveness is very difficult, afraid of getting hurt, one feels indecisive, feel paranoid, sleeplessness, these all are it's symptoms. It is center of spirituality, connecting mind with spirit, compassion for others all is connecting with this chakra. If it is not healed then one is jealous but shows that he is not!!Its color is green and mantra is YAM, healing of this junction is very important, while chanting yam one has to visualize this chakra vibrating with green color.

Throat Chakra : This is located in your throat and this is responsible for your speaking, for expressing yourself, how you express your thoughts and ideas to people, this chakra is of light blue color and it is responsible for your communication skills, self expression and how you project your ideas. If unbalanced then one will be silent, quite, timid, feeling weak, uncomfortable while one has to speak, inability to voice out thoughts in one's mind, you will have thyroid if it is not balanced. To balance it one must chant it's mantra HAM visualizing light blue color. Once it's healed one can express oneself in best way, communication skills are excellent, people love hearing such person.

Third Eye Chakra: This chakra is located in center of our head, between two eye brows, it is responsible for intelligence, intuition, knowledge insight, intuition and it is Indigo in color, if not balanced, it can lead to headaches, blurry vision and eyestrain, to balance it you can chant it's mantra AUM or OM, and visualize it's color Indigo.

Crown Chakra: This chakra is located at center of head so it is called Crown Chakra, It is connected with all other chakras and it's most important chakra for our growth and it connects us with our life purpose, it is source of Divine Wisdom and life force. If one's chakra is balanced that person will have wide vision, open minded, has Divine Connection and ideas, it brings bliss to that person, when it is not balanced that person will be stubborn, narrow minded, skeptical. If this chakra is open then all other chakras are also open and they function perfectly, it's color is violet or white and it's mantra is ahh If we practice chakra meditation daily by these techniques, you will definitely make your life complete, fulfilling and joyful. What I feel personally is that if all adults above 18 years of age start learning and doing chakra healing then no physical or mental ailments will remain on this planet. More and more schools should start adapting these simple ways of life then all your dreams will start manifesting. It's actually a key to happiness, health and fulfillment, each problem on this planet: physical, mental, emotional, or financial is straightaway related to one of seven chakras. One must follow chakra healing and chakra meditation, I am very sure almost every problem in your life will be sorted. What else does one need? Try to learn chakra balancing from an expert my dear readers for happy and fulfilling life and keep doing it daily and you can do it twice thrice or as many times you want to do or do whenever you are irritated or low. You will be amazed at results.

Happy Chakra Healing Guys

Chapter 14

DELIBERATE HAPPINESS

When we read this, we may laugh, how one can create deliberate happiness but when we are ready to receive our dreams in reality, once we move towards way of manifestation, we come to know about Law of Attraction, which is amazing, brings miracles .Then I came to know about vibrations and good vibrations only, are required to fulfill our dreams. One may say that how can our vibrations be good when we are feeling bad!!But my dear friend if you are on your way of fulfilling your dreams, one must understand that nothing can be achieved with low mood or low vibrations. One may ask that what to do when we are in low mood!! Here comes the twist my friend, we have to do practice of pulling ourselves from low mood to some comfort zone, you have to visualize ourselves in a moment of happiness that has already taken place in our life or some future happiness which has to be thought about or visualized, actually one has to train oneself deliberately to be in happy mood to have manifestations. It is deliberate happiness which will null that low moment and recreate a new moment of happiness. When you start doing deliberate happiness technique, you will experience a great bliss and it will bring actual happiness, you may not believe me but you should at least try your hand at it to have beautiful life experiences, It was difficult for me too, in a moment of argument or in a moment of low vibrations, how can one practice deliberate happiness!! It seemed dramatic to me and illogical to my rational mind, but when I did more of manifestations and learnt more about it, I came to know that it's a game of vibrations and high life state, which attracts miracles or fulfillment of your desires into reality. It took me very long to understand it's actual positive outcomes. I actually fell and got up from my own learning, I got up and again tried my hand though my mind refused to accept, but still I tried and wow it happened, by creating happiness or deliberate happiness, I got actual happiness, many arguments became useless and heated conversations became very less then negligent because while in argument with my spouse or family member, I was thinking of a happy moment or visualizing, hahaha, isn't it to be laughed about? But I created my happy moment, created peace, fulfilled dreams, and no fights in family. This deliberate happiness is actually amazing, wonderful tool towards happiness, peace and fulfillment of your dreams. You can try at it by doing it, forgetting to do, again do it, till you master it and once you master it, you will experience total bliss and your own created happiness, which is your own because it's your work, your creation, you have mastered it and reaping it's fruits. After mastering it you will start enjoying its magical effects, once you master it you will experience, when some other people are fighting or feeling low and moving towards depression, you feel that they can change their lives and you know the art but you don't know how to teach them!!But once you start teaching others selflessly you will have beautiful experience yourself, and don't worry about how many will follow you, whoever is ready and willing to learn will learn and of course whose time has come for transformation!!! You do selfless efforts this will add up to your own happiness. Once try your hand at deliberate happiness or at least going to a comfort zone or ease moment at least. Once you start doing it, you will do this magical thing again and again, give it a try at least!! Actually Universe gives you what you give it, It knows and understands only vibrations, if we give bad vibes it will return us same in form of more low moments, if we give it happy vibe it is bound to return more happy vibes to us. Happy creation my friends.

Chapter 15

The Art Of Visualization: we visualize in our thoughts what we want for ourselves, for example our dream car or house, in order to tune into the frequency of one's dream one has to visualize it by sitting and feeling as if you already have it, by doing this you will achieve it faster. We have to feel, believe, think about it then take action towards it. By doing these all you will attract it faster.

Step 1- Your dream should be clear and specific, if you want a car, you should be clear about it's color, model, and time when you want it. We can't confuse Universe by changing our thoughts again and again. One must be totally sure about your choice and then you should act on it. We can do one thing that we can first write about it in a dairy so that we can be more clear and specific about it, after writing about it, we can read it 3-4 times so that you easily memorize it,

Step2- Relax before and after visualization, simply use relaxation as a tool. Before visualization take deep breaths to make your mind relaxed because visualization will be fulfilled if you are in ease mode because in anxiety no manifestation take place, for this one must have relaxed mind.

You have to add emotions with it, like you have to feel that happy emotion as if that thing has already been achieved, if you are visualizing a car, you have to think as if you have already that car, you have to actually feel how would you feel if you actually owned that car, that happiness and proud feeling you would feel while driving that car. That feeling of happiness will bring that car to you, this is law of Universe that it manifests what is given to it, if we give a feeling of anxiety, it returns that, the more real you feel for your car or your dream, faster it will be given back to you. Like for a home you have to visualize it's color, place, how many rooms it has, what kind of furniture, even

Color of sofa, garden, flowers in it, minutest detail one has to see to actually make it happen. Your energy vibrates at same level which is required for Universe to bring it to a reality !! Once it is done, it is drawn to you in actual.

Another point is that one must be thankful or be in gratitude in advance to get it manifested in reality. One must say thank you to Universe as if you already have it, as we already discussed in previous chapter that power of gratitude is very vast and it has many benefits because gratitude attracts more things in our life which we desire, just by being grateful we can attract many things which seem far away from us. So make gratitude a part of life.

Visualization should be done at least at two times daily, before sleeping and after waking up to make manifestation take place faster. Happy fulfilled dreams my dear friends. Many people have benefitted from it and yet many are getting it. Why not be one of them?

Why some times visualization does not work? Because after doing visualization, we send it doubt energy, and lose the chance of getting it fulfilled, at one moment we give it technique of visualization another minute we give it energy of fear or doubt, whether it will happen or not, at that moment only, we lose the game of manifestation. I suggest relax, visualize, say thanks and leave it at its perfect time of reaping. It is going to be fulfilled if you do it daily with emotions of as if you have already received it. More feelings you attach with your visualization more you will get it faster. I will wish all of you to fulfill all your dreams as fast as you start doing all above techniques.

Author's Note

I would suggest all my readers to receive all the blessings of Universe and your Guardian Angels, but I would suggest that read each chapter twice and follow each simple tool, it may seem very tiny tool at the moment but each tool has actually played a vital role in changing my life and I want you all to experience bliss, happiness, peace and joy of reaping fruits of your efforts, but my friend you will have to consciously do the efforts and gradually change your habits from being lazy to being aware and follow all above doable steps. You will start relishing journey of your life. If you want tingling sensation of fulfilling your dreams, dipped in peace and happiness in family life and work life, what else is required!!!

HAPPY AND SELF HEALING LIFE AHEAD IF YOU USE THESE TOOLS CONSISTANTLY

www.ingramcontent.com/pod-product-compliance
Lightning Source LLC
LaVergne TN
LVHW041547070526
838199LV00046B/1858